CONTENTS

Abbreviations km stands for kilometres • **m** stands for metres • **ft** stands for feet • **km/h** stands for kilometres per hour • **mph** stands for miles per hour

All a-board

Any half-decent skateboarder can show off with a few tricks – but what do the top riders do? They make their stunts bigger and better than anyone else's!

Skateboard stunts are a battle between rider and science. As soon as a skater and board get off the ground, **gravity** does its best to pull them back down again. Gravity will always win – but there are ways of making it wait. Big ramps help riders to travel higher and faster, so gravity takes longer to drag them back to earth with a crunch.

Clear air

The Big Air skateboard competition features riders using a 19-metre (62-foot) tall ramp called the Mega Ramp.

Danny Way clears the Great Wall of China on a skateboard in 2005.

Look out below!

He performed several 360° turns in mid-air.

Danny reached speeds of over 80 km/h (50 mph).

---

gravity a force that attracts objects to each other, especially towards Earth

EXTREME

Stunts

Life-threatening Stunt Spectaculars

Paul Harrison

Produced for A & C Black by
Monkey Puzzle Media Ltd
48 York Avenue
Hove BN3 1JD, UK

Published by A & C Black Publishers Limited
36 Soho Square, London W1D 3QY

Paperback published 2010
First published 2009
Copyright © 2009 A & C Black Publishers Limited

ISBN 978-1-4081-1263-2 (hardback)
ISBN 978-1-4081-1986-0 (paperback)

Editor: Susie Brooks
Design: Mayer Media Ltd
Picture research: Lynda Lines
Series consultants: Jane Turner and James de Winter

This book is produced using paper that is made from wood grown in managed, sustainable forests. It is natural, renewable and recyclable. The logging and manufacturing processes conform to the environmental regulations of the country of origin.

Printed in Malaysia by Tien Wah Press (Pte.) Ltd

Picture acknowledgements
Alamy p. 26–27 (Jacob Ammentorp Lund); Bigfoot 4X4 Inc p. 9 top; Corbis pp. 1 (CSPA/NewSport), 4–5 (Jason Lee/Reuters), 12 top (CSPA/NewSport), 21 (Hulton-Deutsch Collection), 24 left (Hulton-Deutsch Collection); Discovery Films/BBC p. 15; Getty Images pp. 6, 14, 17 (Colin Meagher), 18–19 (AFP), 22–23, 28 left (AFP); MPM Images pp. 5 top, 10; PA Photos p. 23 (François Mori/AP); Photolibrary.com pp. 20 (Sundell Joakim), 28–29 (Max Dereta); Reuters p. 11 (Brendan McDermid); Rex Features pp. 7 bottom (ITV), 8–9 (Kip Rano), 12–13 (Everett Collection), 24–25 (EDPICS/Bill Smith); Ronald Grant Archive p. 7 top; Sony Pics/Everett p. 26 left; Topfoto.co.uk pp. 16 (ImageWorks), 18 (UPP).

The front cover shows a stuntman performing at the World Stunt Awards in Los Angeles, USA (Corbis/Mario Anzuoni/Reuters).

Every effort has been made to contact copyright holders of material reproduced in this book. Any omissions will be rectified in subsequent printings if notice is given to the publishers.

500 m (1,600 ft) down!

Danny flew 24 m (79 ft) high over the wall.

▲ Bob Burnquist **grinds** along a rail into the Grand Canyon in 2006. He is wearing a parachute for a safe landing.

Even the cops were fascinated!

Danny used a huge ramp to give him enough energy to get over the wall.

grind to ride a skateboard down a rail

Silent stars

Modern movie stunts look really extreme thanks to computer trickery. But, in the early days of film there were no computers to help out. All the stunts were done for real!

It looks as if Harold Lloyd is hanging high over the street – but the camera angle hides a ledge just below him.

An old-fashioned stunt was a bit like a magic trick – the idea was not to let the audience see how it was done. Silent movie stars such as Buster Keaton and Harold Lloyd knew how to make stunts work. Clever planning and **camera angles** were the keys to making a stunt look much more dangerous than it really was.

Gulp!

Thrillers!

Harold Lloyd's films became known as "thrill comedies" thanks to his extreme stunts.

camera angle the position of a camera in relation to the subject

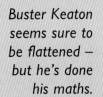

Buster Keaton seems sure to be flattened — but he's done his maths.

Keaton has measured the height of the window.

This tells him exactly how far away to stand.

Keaton stands exactly where the open window lands.

Phew!

Leaping loonies

Motorbikes and monster trucks aren't meant to fly – but that doesn't stop people from trying to get them airborne!

Stunt rider Evel Knievel jumps a row of London buses in 1975.

The angle of the take-off ramp and the power of the engine give the bike speed.

Gravity pulls the bike downwards.

airborne carried through the air

With enough speed and a ramp, even monster trucks can fly.

If it goes wrong, the bike lands here.

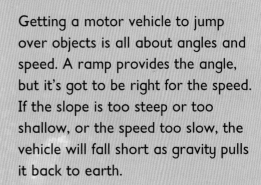

Getting a motor vehicle to jump over objects is all about angles and speed. A ramp provides the angle, but it's got to be right for the speed. If the slope is too steep or too shallow, or the speed too slow, the vehicle will fall short as gravity pulls it back to earth.

Long jumper!

In March 2008, Robbie Maddison jumped a whopping 107 metres (346 feet) on a motorbike – a new world record.

Water torture

Harry Houdini amazed audiences with his scary underwater escape tricks.

Holding your breath for a long time underwater feels like torture. Your lungs fill with carbon dioxide, and it's only a matter of time before you fall unconscious. How long do you think you could last for?

Most people can hold their breath for no more than a minute. But some performers and **free divers** can last much longer than this. They train themselves in special techniques, such as drawing **oxygen** from other parts of the body towards the lungs. Staying calm also helps people to use less oxygen – but that's difficult when you know you could possibly drown.

Staying underwater

If divers gulp pure oxygen – known as oxygen loading – before they dive, they can stay underwater for longer.

carbon dioxide waste gas we breathe out   **free divers** people who dive without air tanks

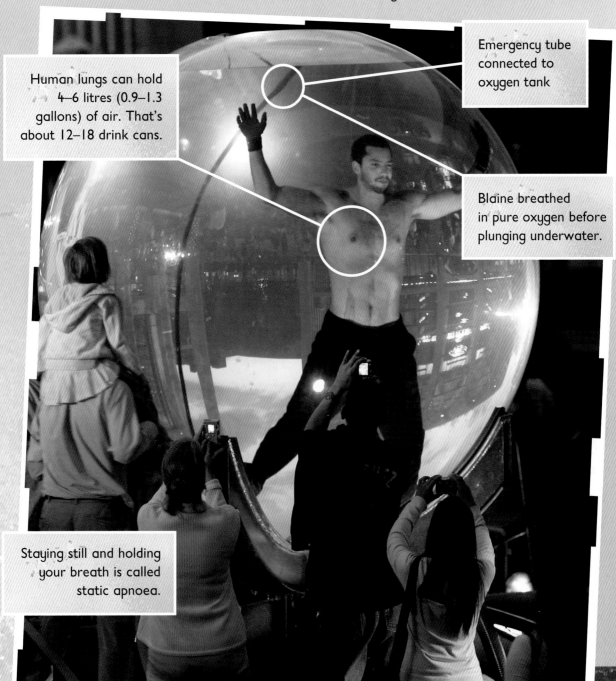

Emergency tube connected to oxygen tank

Human lungs can hold 4–6 litres (0.9–1.3 gallons) of air. That's about 12–18 drink cans.

Blaine breathed in pure oxygen before plunging underwater.

Staying still and holding your breath is called static apnoea.

oxygen gas that humans need for survival

Crazy cars

If your car skidded, spun or rolled over on to its roof then you'd fail your driving test – but this is everyday work for a stunt driver.

"Spiderman" jumps from one car to the other.

Balancing on two wheels is difficult because you are driving on such a thin strip of tyre.

Don't brake!

A lot of stunt driving is about keeping going. If you don't, gravity gets the better of you and pulls you down to the ground.

The average family car weighs around 1,500 kilograms (3,300 pounds) and is designed to drive on four wheels — but that doesn't mean it has to. Cars can jump 60 metres (200 feet) over obstacles, do **barrel rolls** in mid-air and even go skiing — that's whizzing along on two wheels, not the winter sport!

James Bond performs his famous barrel roll stunt in The Man with the Golden Gun.

The perfect speed is needed to complete the jump and the turn.

GRAVITY

barrel roll where the car spins upside down then the right way up in mid-air

High jinks

Imagine tiptoeing across a wire that's narrower than your foot – with nothing either side and a knee-knocking drop below. Welcome to the world of tightrope walking!

People have walked tightropes in the most extreme locations – across **ravines**, between skyscrapers and even over Niagara Falls. At King's Island, Ohio, in the USA, a record-breaking walker managed 609 metres (2,000 feet) across a high wire. Long tightropes like this wobble and sag, making it much harder to keep your balance. Stumble and there's only one way to go – down.

Tightrope-walking legend Charles Blondin crosses Niagara Falls carrying his manager, Harry Colcord, on his back.

Fun times

The correct name for tightrope walking is funambulism.

ravine a deep, narrow valley between two cliffs

In 1974, Philippe Petit walked between two skyscrapers in New York wearing the world's biggest flares!

Crosswinds make balancing more difficult.

Petit's stunt lasted for 45 minutes.

GRAVITY

A pole helps Petit to balance.

crosswinds winds that blow from the side

Over the edge

Big waterfalls look spectacular and are supremely dangerous – so why would anyone want to float over the edge of one?

Going over the edge of a waterfall isn't difficult – the hard part is surviving. Large waterfalls can drop over 30 metres (100 feet) into churning waters and dangerous **currents** below. But whooshing over falls in a barrel or **kayak** isn't as mad as it seems. Both are **buoyant**, meaning they will quickly float back up to the surface – and you've more chance of living if you don't sink too far.

Annie Edson Taylor was the first person to go over Niagara Falls in a barrel – aged 63!

Whoosh!

More than 168,000 cubic metres (6 million cubic feet) of water rush over the crest of Niagara Falls every minute.

current the flow of water   **kayak** a canoe with a covered-over top

Kayaker shoots off waterfall into the air

Water shoots off top of cliff

The kayaker's paddling speed has taken him further out than the water. But he cannot resist gravity for long!

Helmet protects the kayaker in case of a rocky landing.

GRAVITY

Kayak is sealed to lock in air. This makes it lighter than water, so it will bob afloat when it lands.

An extreme sports fan gets his thrills in a waterfall.

buoyant able to float

Free fall

You pay a lot of money to jump out of an aeroplane with a parachute. **But BASE jumpers don't bother with a plane – they just throw themselves from a high object instead.**

There are two more big differences between normal parachuting and BASE jumping. First, surprise crosswinds and **updrafts** can whistle round objects such as cliffs and buildings – and these affect the parachute. Second, BASE jumpers usually have less time to open their chute. Get it wrong, and they won't live to regret it.

BASE jumpers celebrate the opening of the world's tallest building in Taiwan.

All in the name

The letters **BASE** stand for:

B – Buildings

A – Aerials

S – Spans (e.g. bridges)

E – Earth (e.g. mountains)

updraft wind blowing upwards

At this moment, a BASE jumper hopes he's packed his parachute properly!

UPDRAFT

Air resistance stops jumpers from falling any faster than 190 km/h (120 mph).

AIR RESISTANCE

Gravity is stronger than updraft and air resistance put together.

GRAVITY

air resistance the way air slows objects down as they move

The wall of death

Riding a motorbike upside down, or sideways around the walls of a huge barrel, seems impossible – so how do riders defy nature and live to tell the tale?

Wall-of-death rides became popular fairground attractions in the 1930s. Sometimes the riders took passengers with them – imagine being picked out of the crowd for that!

The trick to cheating gravity in the wall of death is simple – sheer speed. As long as the bike is moving fast enough, the rider will not end up in a heap on the floor.

Though it looks dangerous, the hardest thing about riding a globe of death like this is not hitting other people.

Roaring on

Lions, monkeys and bears have all ridden the wall of death as passengers in cars. Wouldn't fancy being the driver...

---

force a push or a pull on an object, making it move or change shape

A daring spectator becomes part of the show in this wall-of-death stunt.

Hello, mum!

Bike's speed produces **force** that pushes the tyres against the wall.

SPEED

GRAVITY

21

Get a grip

When most of us want to get to the top of a building, we use the stairs or a lift. Extreme stunt lovers prefer to climb up the outside – without using ropes!

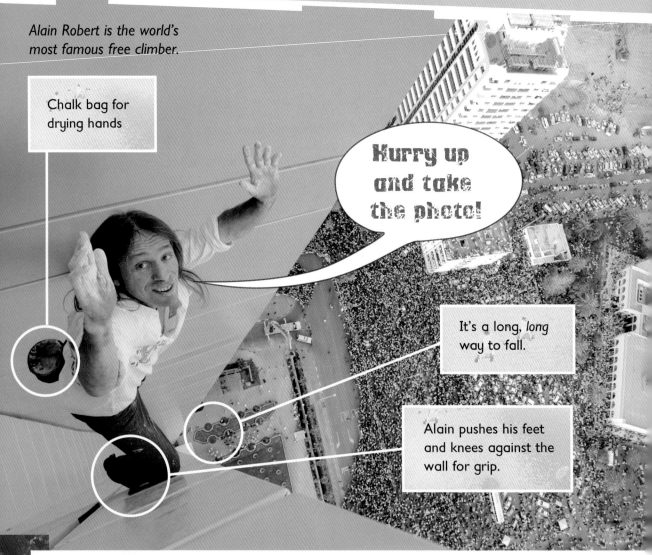

Alain Robert is the world's most famous free climber.

Chalk bag for drying hands

Hurry up and take the photo!

It's a long, *long* way to fall.

Alain pushes his feet and knees against the wall for grip.

vertigo fear of heights   **urban** describes a built-up area, such as a town or city

Don't look down!

Alain Robert has been climbing buildings since 1994. Unbelievably, he claims to suffer from **vertigo**.

FRICTION GRIPS

FRICTION GRIPS

FRICTION GRIPS

FRICTION GRIPS

GRAVITY PULLS

Climbers need good body strength, so that they can hold on.

Scrambling up buildings without using ropes is called **urban** free climbing. Getting a good grip is really important, so sweaty hands are very bad news. Climbers use chalk powder to keep their hands as dry as possible. This gives them some **friction** to prevent a slippery fall.

friction   the force that slows movement between two objects rubbing together

The human cannonball

Cannons are for wars, aren't they? Yes – but some people are so desperate to fly that they are willing to be fired like a cannonball!

BANG! A human cannonball takes to the air.

A spring inside the cannon fires out the cannonball.

Energy carries the cannonball upwards.

Smoke makes the cannon look real.

The human cannonball act is a combination of stunt work and science. Before being blasted through the air, the cannonballs need to know both the angle of their flight and their speed. This tells them how far away to put the catching net. Any messed-up sums and they're in for a painful landing.

Spring loaded

The cannon isn't a real cannon. Rather than using gunpowder to propel the cannonball, a big spring is used.

The human cannonball somersaults in the air to land on his back in the net.

Gravity pulls downwards on the cannonball — and wins in the end!

Cheap thrills

Runner judges the gap.

Running around town is one thing – but some people take it to a whole new level! Free running, or *parkour*, is a sport that doesn't let walls or buildings get in its way.

Free running is all about getting from one place to another – fast. Instead of going round things, the runner jumps, swings or climbs over obstacles. A good sense of balance is essential as many of the moves are acrobatic. **Spatial awareness** is also handy, so runners don't misjudge a gap and fall.

Free running featured in the James Bond film Casino Royale.

spatial awareness knowing where you are in relation to objects around you

Leaping over gaps takes fitness, balance and a good sense of distance and height.

Defeats gravity to head for a perfect landing on the wall.

ENERGY

Runner's arms and legs help him balance in the air.

GRAVITY

Ear ear

A person's balance is controlled by **sensors** inside the ear. That's why ear infections can make people feel dizzy.

sensors things that pick up information such as movement, light or heat

Free as a bird

Skydivers hurtle towards the earth with the aid of their wing suits.

People have often dreamed of soaring through the skies like birds – but we've always needed bulky equipment or aircraft to do it. Until now...

Our arms aren't strong enough to flap wings successfully, but a wing suit can make it feel as if we're flying. A wing suit has cloth panels between the legs and arms, which make the wearer's **surface area** bigger. This increases air resistance, slowing the fall and allowing the person to **glide** like a bird.

Swiss inventor Yves Rossy has developed a jet-powered personal wing, capable of travelling at over 290 km/h (180 mph).

surface area the size of something on the outside

Natural solution

Some animals, such as flying squirrels, have flaps of skin, like a wing suit. This helps them to soar from tree to tree.

Wing suits increase air resistance.

Air resistance slows the fallers...

... but gravity still pulls harder.

glide to fly smoothly through the air without a source of power

Glossary

airborne carried through the air

air resistance the way air slows objects down as they move

barrel roll where the car spins upside down then the right way up in mid-air

buoyant able to float

camera angle the position of a camera in relation to the subject

carbon dioxide the waste gas that we breathe out

crosswinds winds that blow from the side

current the flow of water

force a push or a pull on an object, making it move or change shape

free divers people who dive without air tanks

friction the force that slows movement between two objects rubbing together

glide to fly smoothly through the air without a source of power

gravity a force that attracts objects to each other, especially towards Earth

grind to ride a skateboard down a rail

kayak a canoe with a covered-over top, paddled with a double-bladed oar

oxygen gas that humans need for survival

ravine a deep, narrow valley between two cliffs

sensors things that pick up information such as movement, light or heat

spatial awareness knowing where you are in relation to objects around you

surface area the size of something on the outside

updraft wind blowing upwards

urban describes a built-up area, such as a town or city

vertigo fear of heights

Further information

Books

Deciding which are the best stunts ever attempted could be argued about until the end of time. One author puts down his top ten in **The World's Most Dangerous Stunts** by Tim O'Shei (Edge Books, 2006)

Another book featuring spectacular stunts along with interviews and statistics and facts is **Yikes! Scariest Stunts Ever!** by Jesse Leon McCann (Scholastic, 2006)

Websites

There are loads of websites out there that feature video clips of extreme stunts. Here is a small selection:

www.aerialextreme. com/stock_video
Videos of skydiving stunts and BASE jumping.

www.urbanfreeflow.com
The people who got free running and *parkour* started in the UK organise displays and events and train everyone from school pupils to the armed forces.

http://davidblaine.com
The official site of the American magician and street performer.

www.stuntranch.com
The stunt ranch is an organisation that teaches children and adults about stunts and the science behind them. The site shows clips from some of their shows and suggests some decent-looking books to buy, too.

www.skateparkoftampa. com
A massive skateboarding site covering everything from clothing to videos on how to do tricks.

Films

Ben-Hur directed by William Wyler (MGM, 1959)
A story of revenge set in Roman times. The most famous scene is a thrilling chariot race. There is a rumour that a stuntman actually died filming this scene, but it's not true.

Raiders of the Lost Ark directed by Stephen Spielberg (Paramount Pictures, 1981)
All-action archaeologist Indiana Jones battles the Nazis to get the Ark of the Covenant. There's a famous fight scene on a moving truck.

The World Is Not Enough directed by Michael Apted (MGM, 1999)
Super spy James Bond foils terrorist plots and manages to make a motorboat do a barrel roll in this action-packed thriller.

Index